Alfred's Premier Piano

PERFORMANCE 1B

MW01011442

Dennis Alexander • Gayle Kowalchyk • E. L. Lancaster • Victoria McArthur • Martha Mier

Alfred's *Premier Piano Course* Performance Book 1B includes motivational music in a variety of styles, reinforcing concepts introduced in the Lesson Book 1B. Duet accompaniments further encourage stylistic performances.

The pieces in this book correlate page by page with the materials in Lesson Book 1B. They should be assigned according to the instructions in the upper right corner of each page of this book. They also may be assigned as review material at any time after the student has passed the designated Lesson Book page.

A compact disc recording is included with this book. It can serve as a *performance* model or as a *practice* companion. See information about the CD on page 32. A General MIDI disk (23259) is available separately.

Performance skills and musical understanding are enhanced through *Premier Performer* suggestions. Students will enjoy performing these pieces for family and friends in a formal recital or on special occasions. See the List of Compositions on page 32.

Edited by Morton Manus

Cover Design by Ted Engelbart
Interior Design by Tom Gerou
Illustrations by Jimmy Holder
Music Engraving by Linda Lusk

2

The Spelling Bee

Use with Alfred's Premier Piano Course,
Lesson Book 1B, page 7

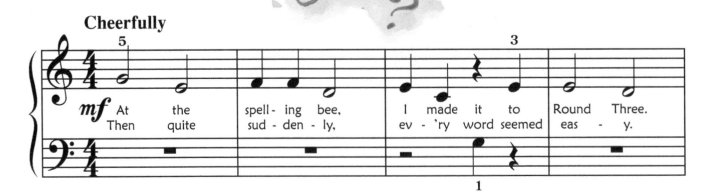

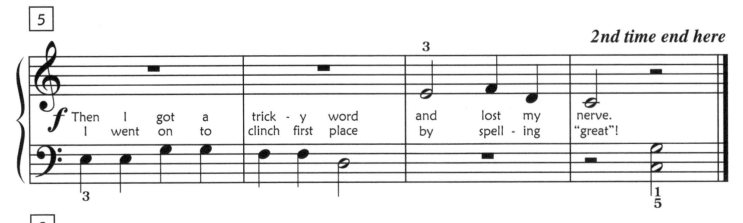

Duet: Student plays one octave higher.

Premier Performer

Keep a steady beat when the melody changes hands.

Mary Ann

Lesson Book: pages 8–9

Happily, with a beat

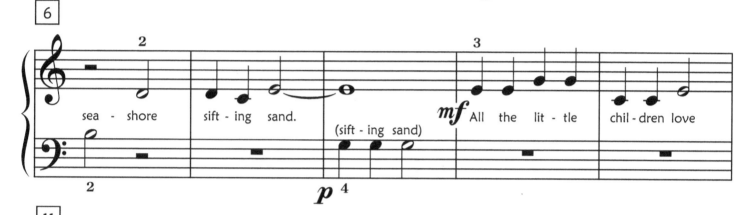

Duet: Student plays one octave higher.

Premier Performer — *Play the LH softly in measures 4, 8, 12 and 16.*

Lesson Book: page 11

Our Team Will Play Tonight

With confidence

Duet: Student plays one octave higher.

9

e - ven if we're be - hind, and things look grim.

13

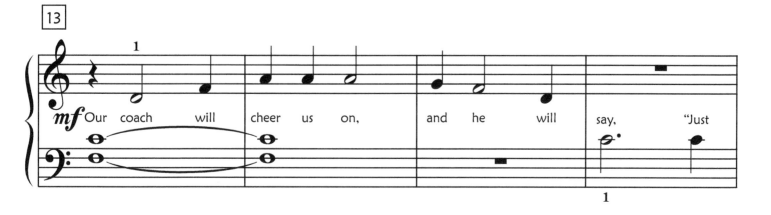

mf Our coach will cheer us on, and he will say, "Just

17

keep on try - ing, do your best, *f* you know the way!

21

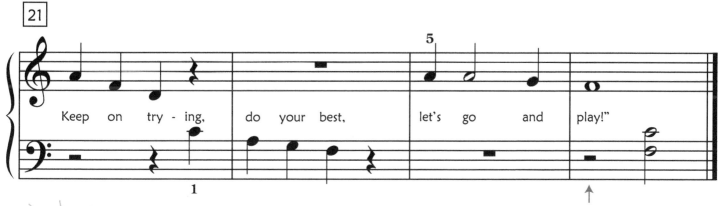

Keep on try - ing, do your best, let's go and play!"

Press damper pedal and hold to end.

Premier Performer *Before playing, tap both hands and count aloud measures 1–2, then measures 5–6.*

Lesson Book: page 14

The County Fair

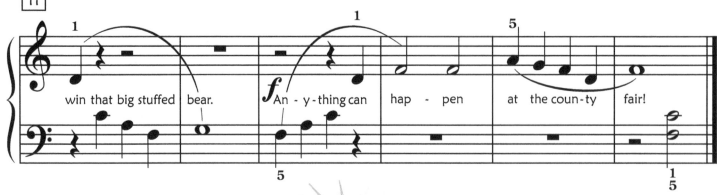

Premier Performer

Play the melody legato when it moves from one hand to the other.

Duet: Student plays one octave higher.

Lesson Book: page 15

The Tennis Match

Looking right and looking left— watching ten-nis hurts my neck! Back and forth I

watch the ball till I can't turn my head at all! When the ball goes in the net,

then I get a lit-tle rest. Tell me, please, what is the score, be - cause my neck is get-ting sore!

Premier Performer

Circle all dynamic signs and remember to use them when you play.

Duet: Student plays one octave higher.

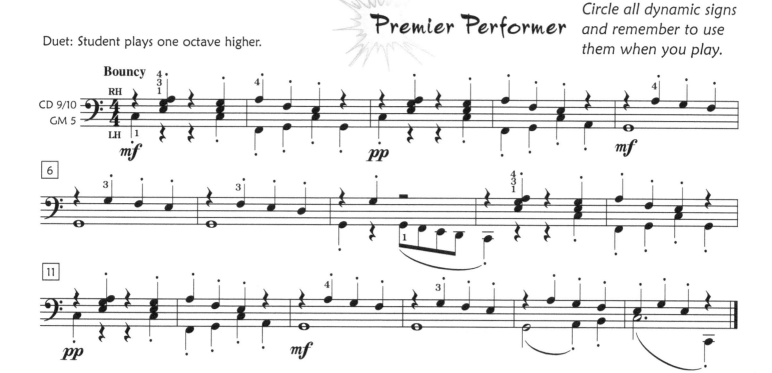

CD 9/10
GM 5

Lesson Book: page 19

Fourth Grade Band

Lively

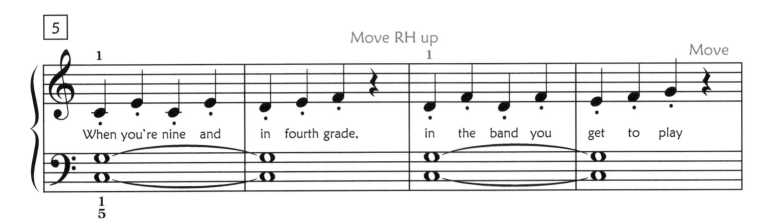

5

Move RH up

When you're nine and in fourth grade, in the band you get to play

9

Move

an - y in - stru - ment you choose— trum - pet, tu - ba or the flute.

13 *Play RH 1 octave higher to end*

Move   Move

Would you play the pic - co - lo? Read the high notes, not the low.

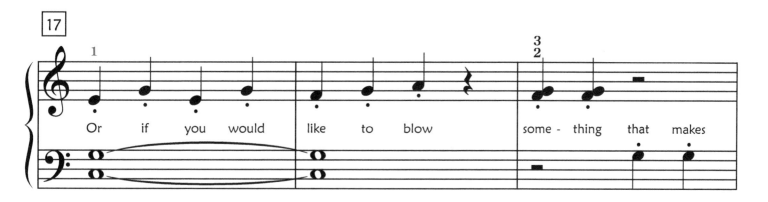

Or if you would like to blow some - thing that makes

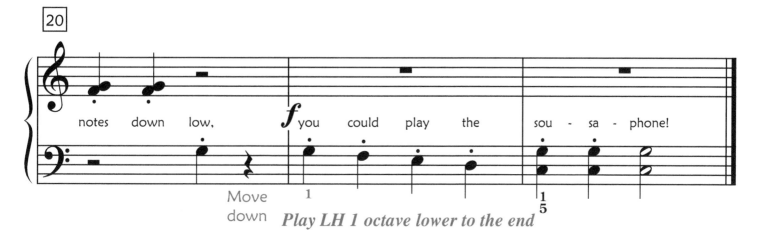

notes down low, *f* you could play the sou - sa - phone!

Move
down **Play LH 1 octave lower to the end**

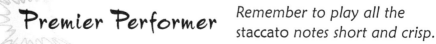

Premier Performer   Remember to play all the
staccato *notes short and crisp.*

10

Winter Waltz

Lesson Book: page 21

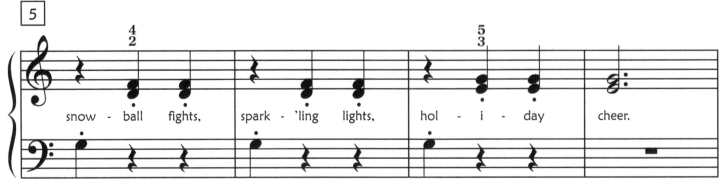

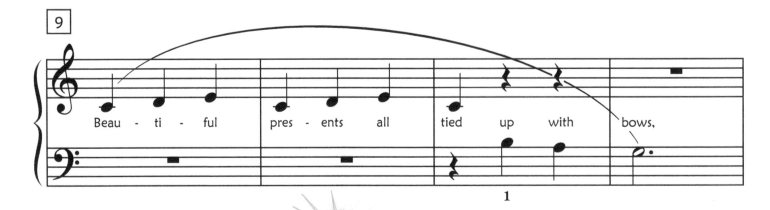

Duet: Student plays one octave higher.

Premier Performer *Play the notes under the slurs very legato.*

Lesson Book: page 22

Mexican Clapping Song
(Chiapanecas)

CD 15/16   GM 8

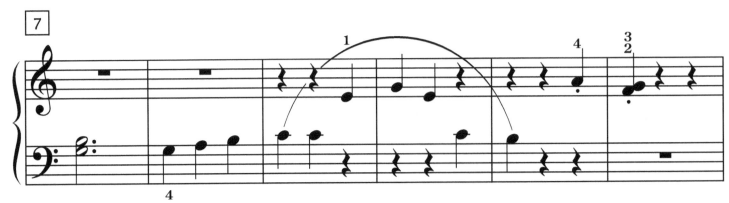

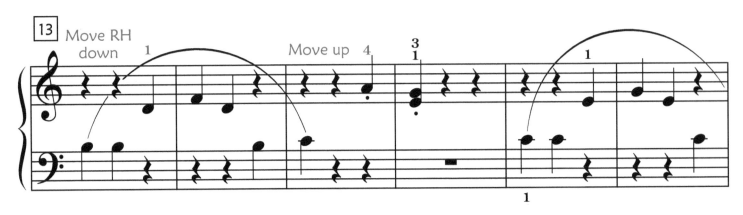

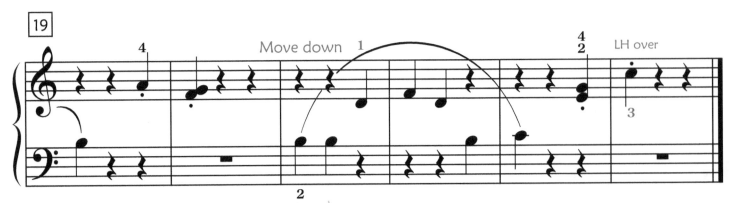

Premier Performer

Play a little louder on the first beat of each measure.

Summer Vacation

Moderate waltz tempo

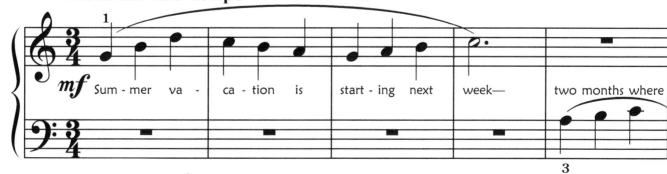

Sum - mer va - ca - tion is start - ing next week— two months where

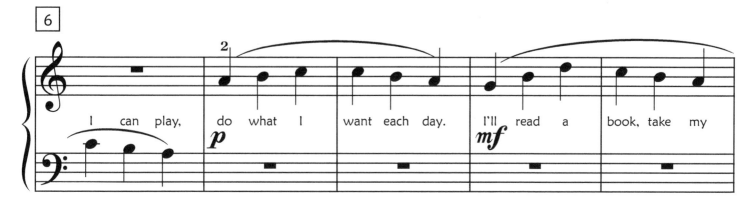

I can play, do what I want each day. I'll read a book, take my

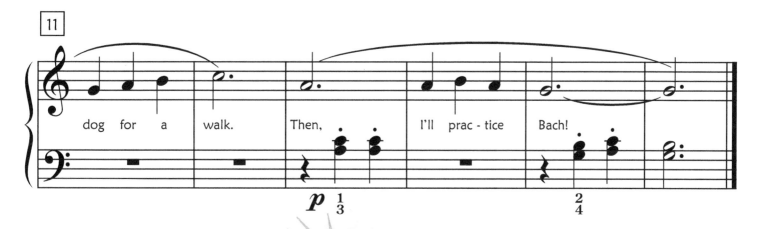

dog for a walk. Then, I'll prac - tice Bach!

Duet: Student plays one octave higher.

Premier Performer   *Play the harmonic intervals softly in measures 13, 15–16.*

Moderate waltz tempo

CD 17/18
GM 9

I Just Love Pizzazz!

Lesson Book: page 25

I just love piz - zazz, all that razz - ma - tazz,

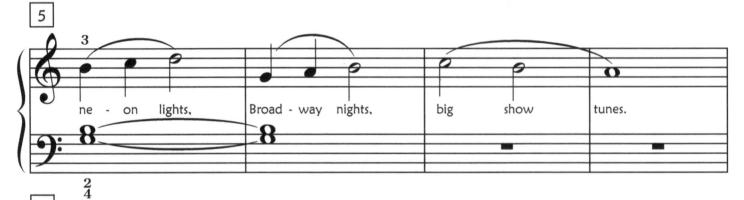

ne - on lights, Broad - way nights, big show tunes.

When the mu - sic plays, and the danc - ers sway,

Duet: Student plays one octave higher.

Premier Performer

Play the LH melody with firm, strong fingers.

CD 19/20
GM 10

Scottish Plaid

Lesson Book: page 29

CD 21/22   GM 11

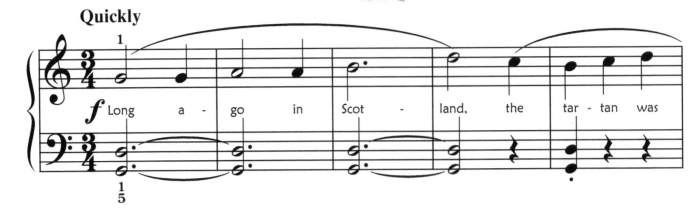

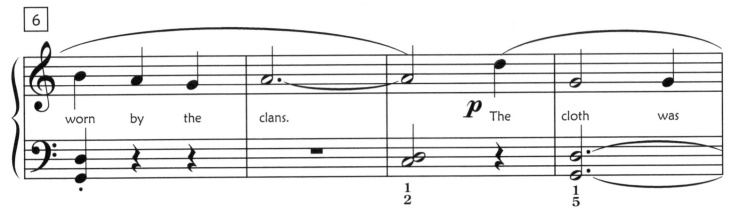

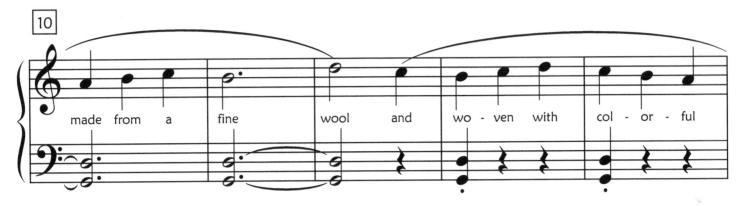

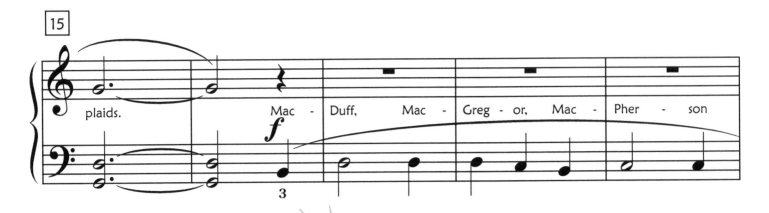

Premier Performer

Imagine the sound of Scottish bagpipes as you play the LH.

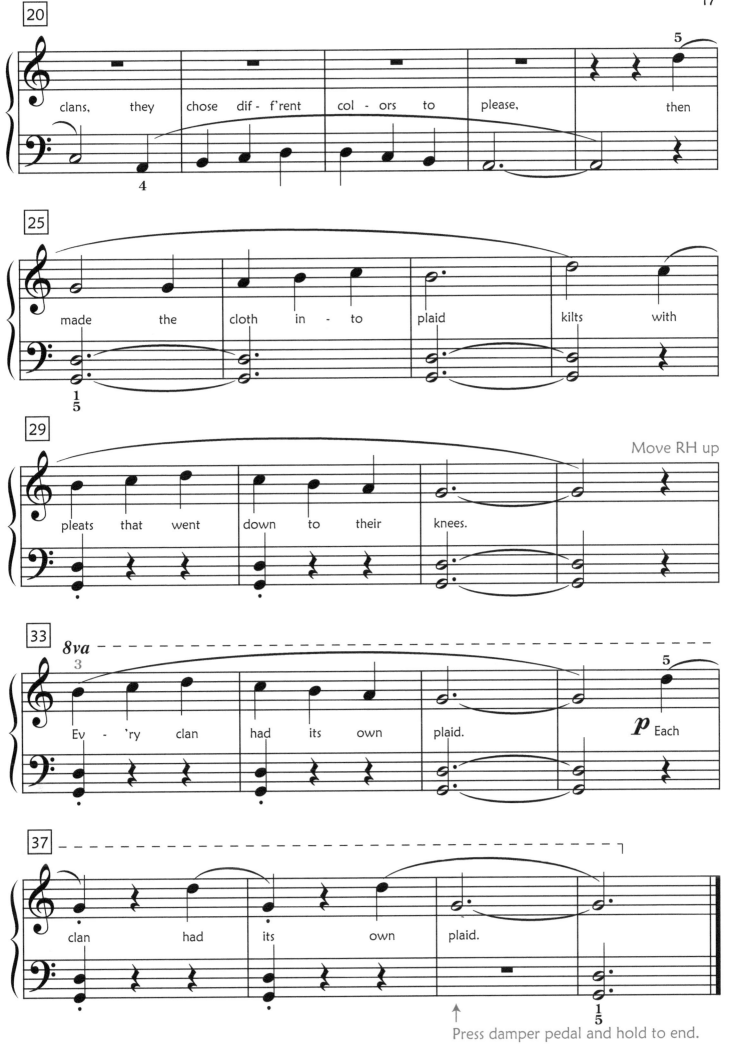

As Morning Dawns

Lesson Book: page 31

CD 23/24   GM 12

Slowly

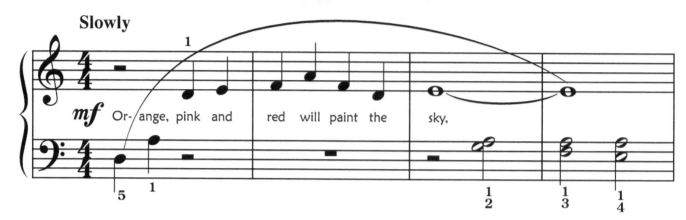

mf Or- ange, pink and red will paint the sky,

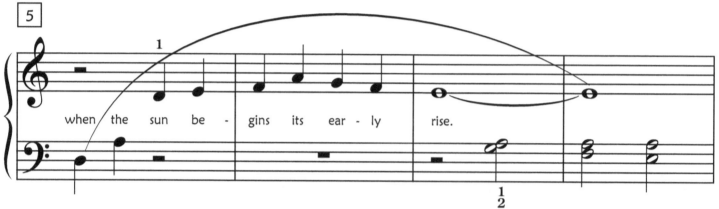

5

when the sun be - gins its ear - ly rise.

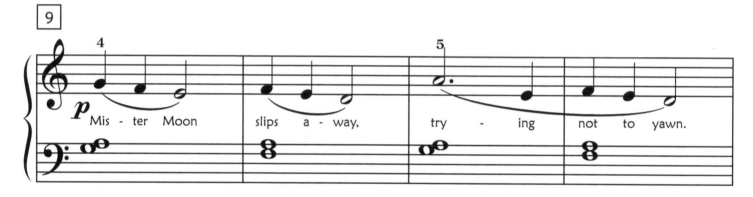

9

p Mis - ter Moon slips a - way, try - ing not to yawn.

13

mf Day will break, earth will wake *rit.* as morn - ing dawns.

Premier Performer   *Play the LH harmonic intervals softer than the RH melody.*

Press damper pedal and hold to end.

Ancient Dance

Lesson Book: page 32

Duet: Student plays one octave higher.

Premier Performer

Make sure that your hands look like a level tabletop when playing the harmonic 5ths.

20

My Dog

CD 27/28   GM 14

Pogo Stick

CD 29/30   GM 15

Moderately fast

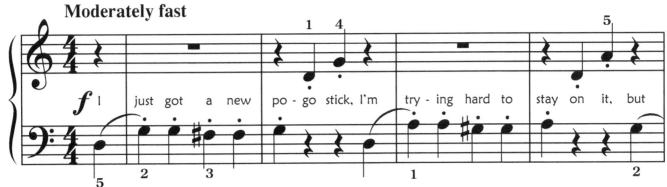

f I just got a new po - go stick, I'm try - ing hard to stay on it, but

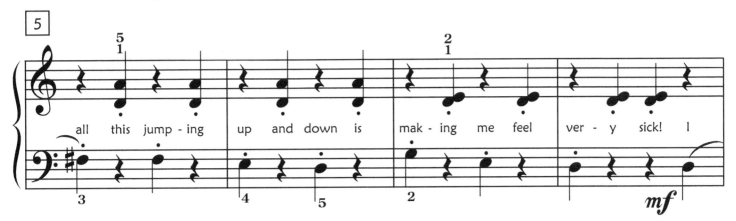

all this jump - ing up and down is mak - ing me feel ver - y sick! I

mf

won - der if my mom and dad would let me stop (they might be glad) so I could trade it

gradually softer   Move RH *8va*- - - - - - - -
up

in for some - thing that is nice and still so that I *p* will not feel so ill. *f* Please!

Move LH
down

Premier Performer   *Play the staccato quarter notes bouncy, like a pogo stick.*

22

Square Dance!

Lesson Book: page 38

Swing your part - ner round 'n' round, till her feet are off the ground.

It's time to do - si - do, kick heels up, tap your toes.

Move RH *8va*
up

Move   Move

Premier Performer

Circle each staccato dot and remember to play these notes short and crisp.

Duet: Student plays one octave higher.

CD 31/32
GM 16

Snake Charmer

CD 33/34   GM 17

Mysteriously

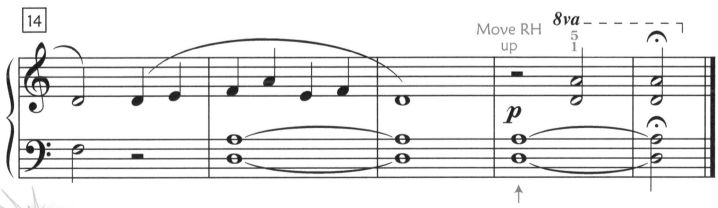

Premier Performer   *Slightly lift your hands for rests.*

Move RH up

Press damper pedal and hold to end.

When the Saints Go Marching In

March-like

f Oh, when the · saints · go march-ing · in, · oh, when the

Premier Performer · *Always play the LH softer than the RH.*

Duet: Student plays one octave higher.

Lesson Book: page 43

Scarborough Fair

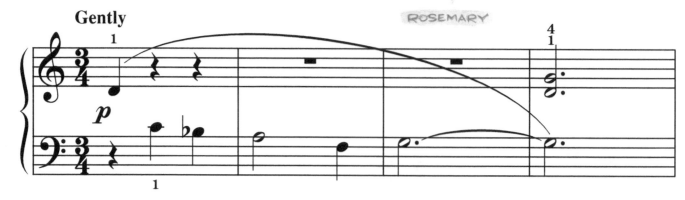

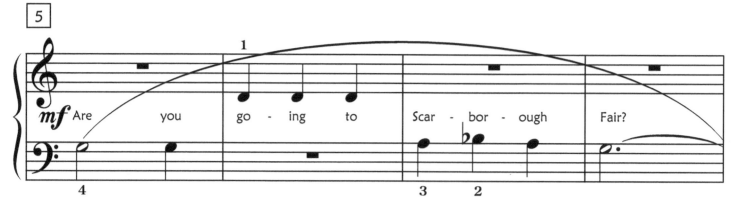

Duet: Student plays one octave higher.

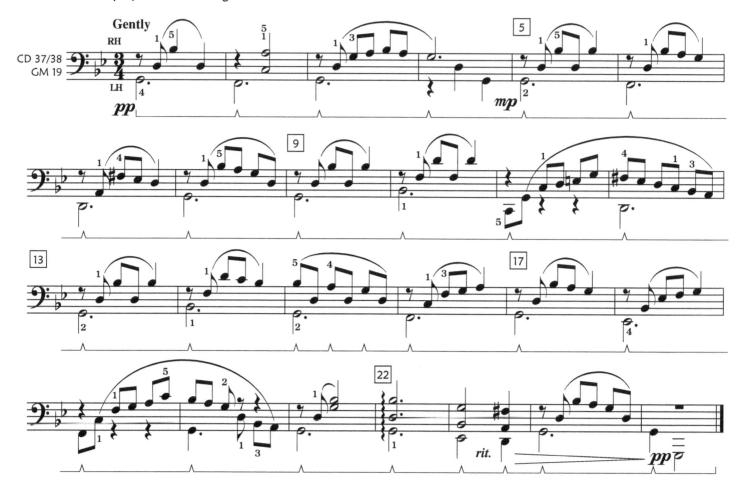

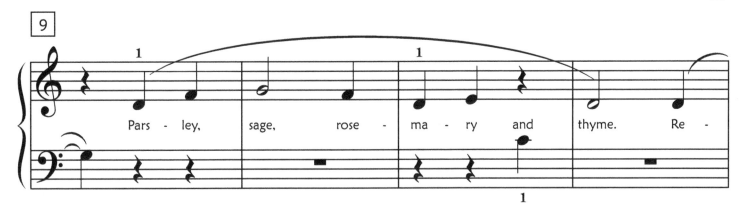

9

Pars - ley, sage, rose - ma - ry and thyme. Re -

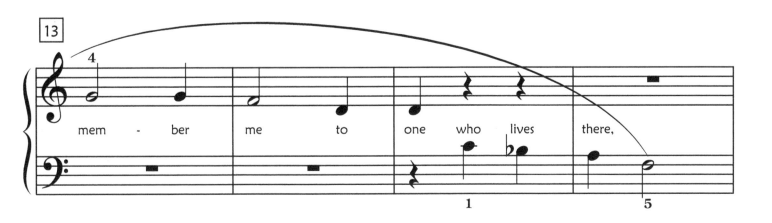

13

mem - ber me to one who lives there,

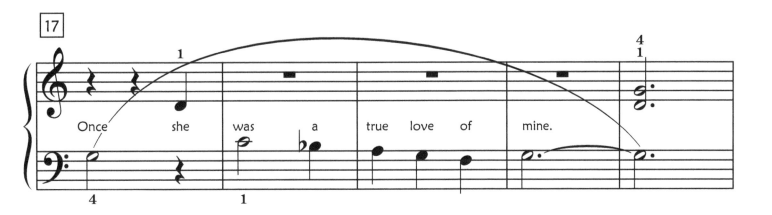

17

Once she was a true love of mine.

22

Move RH up   8va

gradually softer
rit.

p

↑
Press damper pedal and hold to end.

Premier Performer   *Play the melody with a beautiful singing tone.*

28

I Eat My Peas with Honey

Moderately fast

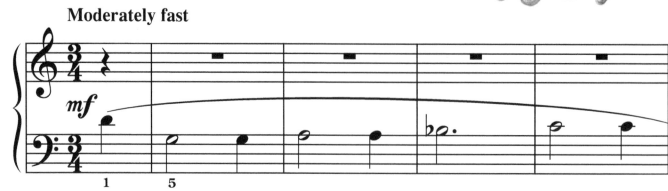

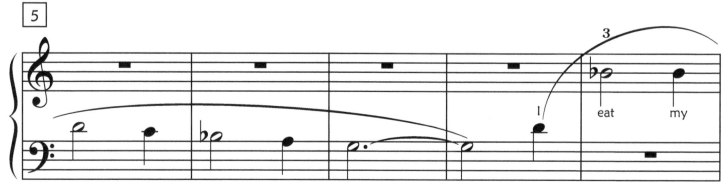

Premier Performer

*Silently "play" measures 25–32
to become skilled at the moves.*

Duet: Student plays one octave higher.

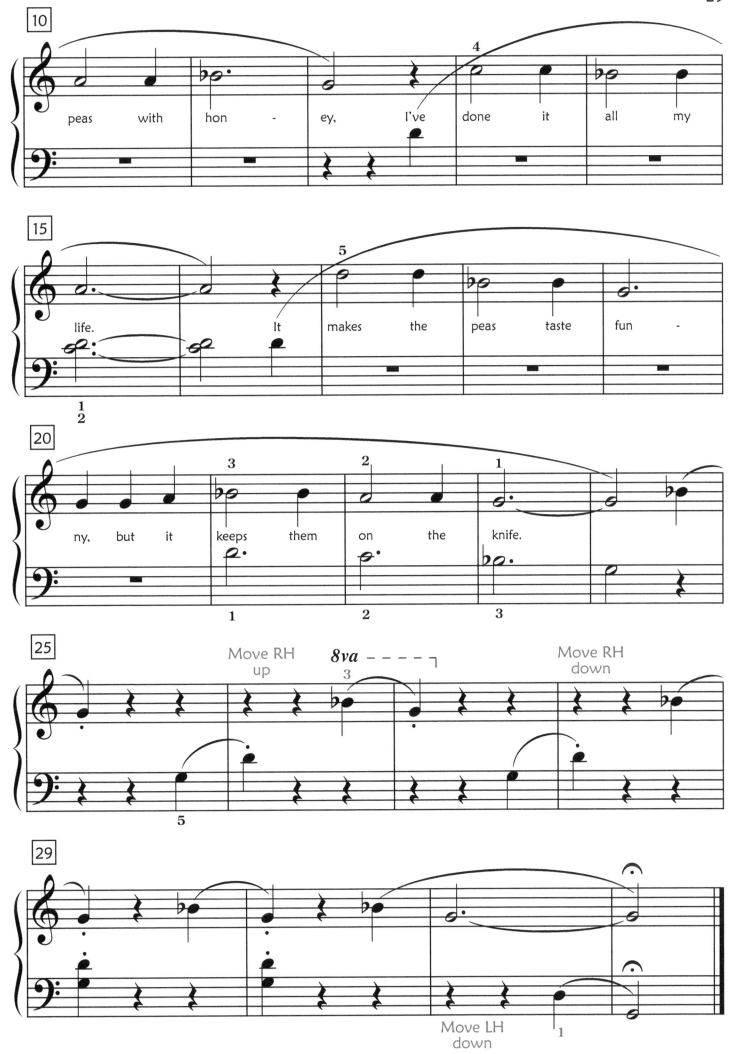

Lesson Book: pages 46–47

I Love to Play Piano!

CD 41/42   GM 21

Fast and rhythmic

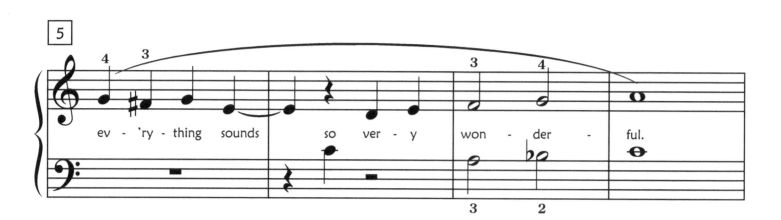

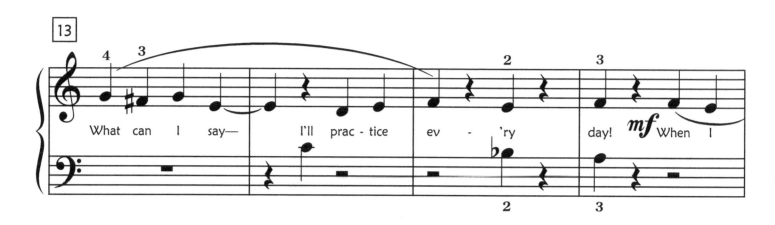

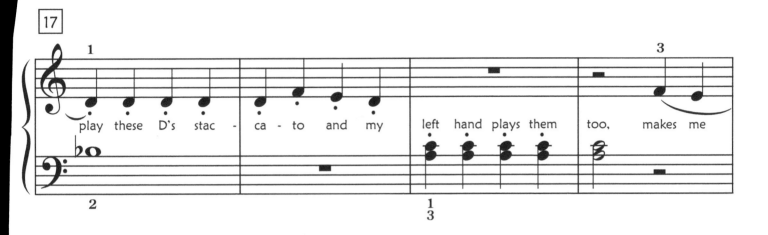

17

play these D's stac - ca - to and my left hand plays them too, makes me

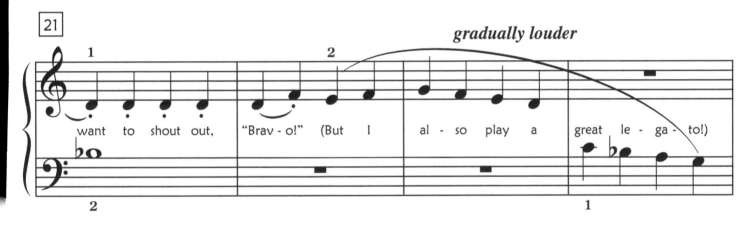

21

gradually louder

want to shout out, "Brav - o!" (But I al - so play a great le - ga - to!)

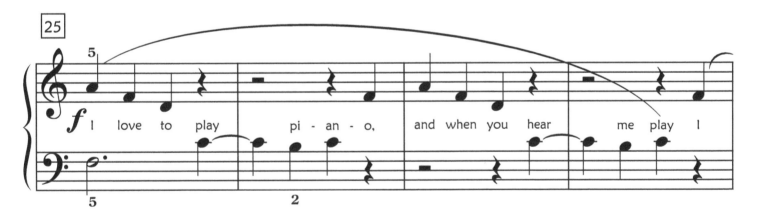

25

f I love to play pi - an - o, and when you hear me play I

29

hope you will stand and shout, "Hoo - ray!" O - K!

Premier Performer *Confidently play the legato and staccato notes.*

List of Compositions

*MP3 files of audio performances on acoustic piano and orchestrated accompaniments are available for download at **alfred.com/ppcperformance1b**. There are four versions of each piece:*

*1. A digitally orchestrated accompaniment **with** piano.*

*2. A digitally orchestrated accompaniment **without** piano.*

*3. A **practice tempo** performed on acoustic piano.*

*4. A **performance tempo** performed on acoustic piano.*

TNT 2 Custom Mix Software, also available for download at the link listed above, allows the user to change tempos in these audio files. In addition, General MIDI files are available for download. These recordings add musical interest and motivate students in the lesson and during practice.

	Track	Page
Ancient Dance	13	19
As Morning Dawns	12	18
County Fair, The	4	6
Fourth Grade Band	6	8
I Eat My Peas with Honey	20	28
I Just Love Pizzazz!	10	14
I Love to Play Piano!	21	30
Mary Ann	2	3
Mexican Clapping Song	8	12
My Dog	14	20
Our Team Will Play Tonight	3	4
Pogo Stick	15	21
Scarborough Fair	19	26
Scottish Plaid	11	16
Snake Charmer	17	23
Spelling Bee, The	1	2
Square Dance!	16	22
Summer Vacation	9	13
Tennis Match, The	5	7
When the Saints Go Marching In	18	24
Winter Waltz	7	10

TNT 2 Software Instructions

To install the TNT 2 software, double-click on the installer file. Once it is installed, you will be able to slow down or speed up each MP3, loop playback, and select specific sections for practicing.

TNT 2 System Requirements:

Windows
10, 8, 7, Vista, XP
QuickTime 7.6.7 or higher
1.8 GHz processor or faster
330 MB hard drive space, 2 GB RAM minimum
Speakers or headphones
Internet access required for updates

Macintosh
OS X 10.4 or higher (Intel only)
QuickTime 7.6.7 or higher
450 MB hard drive space, 2 GB RAM minimum
Speakers or headphones
Internet access for updates

Windows is a registered trademark or trademark of Microsoft Corporation in the United States and/or other countries. Macintosh, OS X and QuickTime are trademarks of Apple Inc.

Performances by Scott Price